For Kobe and Flor

With thanks to Sven Cuylaerts and Ilse Van Peer

Copyright © 2022 Clavis Publishing Inc., New York

Originally published as *De bouwvakker* in Belgium and the Netherlands by Clavis Uitgeverij, 2013
English translation from the Dutch by Clavis Publishing Inc., New York

Visit us on the Web at www.clavis-publishing.com.

No part of this publication may be reproduced or stored in a retrieval system,
or transmitted in any form or by any means, electronic, mechanical, photocopying,
recording, or otherwise, without the prior written permission of the publisher,
except in the case of brief quotations embodied in critical articles and reviews.
For information regarding permissions, write to Clavis Publishing, info-US@clavisbooks.com.

Construction Workers and What They Do written and illustrated by Liesbet Slegers

ISBN 978-1-60537-804-6

This book was printed in August 2022 at Nikara, M. R. Štefánika 858/25, 963 01 Krupina, Slovakia.

First Edition
10 9 8 7 6 5 4 3 2 1

Clavis Publishing supports the First Amendment and celebrates the right to read.

Construction Workers

and What They Do

Liesbet Slegers

Clavis

NEW YORK

Construction workers are hard at work on a new house for a family. The daddy wants a big garage, and the mommy would like to have big windows. Their boy really wants a playroom for all his toys . . . What kind of dream house would you build?

safety goggles

earmuffs

A construction worker wears sturdy clothes. His work pants have lots of pockets, and a small bag on his belt stores his smaller tools. It can be rather dangerous on the construction site, so he wears work boots, a helmet, and safety goggles. And when there's a lot of noise, he wears his earmuffs. His gloves help him pick up things like bricks. You can always see him because of his fluorescent vest.

helmet

gloves

fluorescent vest

belt with bag

work pants

work boots

scaffold

ladder

To build a house, a construction worker needs a lot of tools. Some of them are small, like a tape measure, a hammer, a trowel (to lay bricks), and a level (to keep the wall straight). Some of them are big, like a concrete mixer (to make mortar for the bricks), a jackhammer (to break up hard things), and a grinder (to help smooth rough edges). When a construction worker has to work up high, he stands on a scaffold. He sometimes also uses a bulldozer, an excavator, or a crane.

Before the construction worker starts building, he meets with an architect. The architect thinks of what the house will look like on the outside and on the inside. She draws it all on a big house plan and gives it to the construction worker. Together they talk about what needs to be done to make the house strong *and* pretty.

site hut

toilet

The construction worker works outside all day at the construction site.
Often there's a site hut, where he eats and keeps the house plans.
There's also a toilet. Look! Here comes the heavy bulldozer.
The construction worker uses it to get the ground ready to build.
All the trees, bushes, and rocks have to be removed to make room
for the house. The ground also needs to be level, so the house is
straight and sturdy.

The construction worker now builds the house as it's drawn on the plan. First he measures everything precisely. He uses his tape measure, stakes, and string lines so he knows exactly where all the walls should go. He even has a special surveying machine that measures perfectly! Special barriers are used for fencing off the grounds, because no one can enter the construction site.

Now that the construction worker knows where all the walls will be, it's the big excavator's turn. Before a firm layer of concrete can be poured to support the house, the excavator pulls away some dirt and puts it in a dump truck. The box that holds the dirt is called the dump body. The dump body can tilt, so the driver can empty the whole container out quickly. It would take him ages to scoop all the dirt out with a shovel!

Once the concrete has set, the construction worker builds
concrete blocks where the walls will go. The brick walls will
lean on the concrete blocks. After that, the big concrete mixer
pours a thick layer of concrete carefully between the blocks.
It gets even firmer with a layer of iron mesh in between.
The construction worker spreads the concrete evenly.
When it's dry, it'll be super strong!

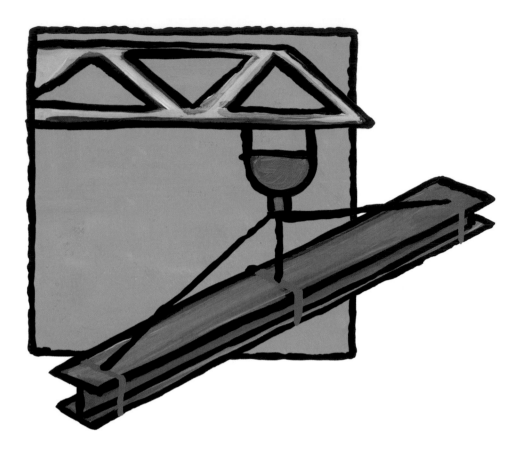

Now the building can really begin. The big crane lifts a package of bricks and takes them to the right place. The small concrete mixer is used to make mortar. The construction worker smears mortar between the bricks with the trowel to make them stick together. When the ground floor is done, the crane lays the heavy iron beams in the right place. It's going to be a strong house!

On the outside of the house, two walls are built side by side.
The construction worker puts insulation between them.
That's a special layer that keeps the house warm in the winter
and makes sure it stays cool in the summer. With a level,
the construction worker makes sure everything is straight so
that the windows and doors will fit in perfectly. If the weather
is very bad, the construction workers stay dry in the site hut,
with a warm cup of coffee.

The building is done, but of course, lots of things still need to be completed before the family can move into their new house! The carpenter makes the wooden frame for the roof. The roofer puts the shingles on it. The construction worker cuts the windows and doors to size. When all that's done, the outside of the house is ready.

The house is finally finished.
The family can move in now!
It was a lot of work, but the result is beautiful.
The boy made a drawing for the construction worker
and gets to try on his helmet. Maybe you would like
to build houses one day too . . .